Life and Times

Queen Elizabeth I

Peggy Burns

WAYLAND

Titles in the Life and Times series:

Florence Nightingale · Queen Elizabeth I · Queen Victoria · William Shakespeare ·

Editor: Liz Gogerly
Consultant: Norah Granger
Cover designer: Jan Sterling
Designer: Joyce Chester
Production controller: Carol Stevens

First published in 1999 by Wayland Publishers Limited
61 Western Road, Hove, East Sussex BN3 1JD

British Cataloguing in Publication Data
Burns, Peggy
    Elizabeth I. – (Life and times)
    1. Elizabeth I, Queen of England, 1533-1603 –
    Juvenile literature
    2. Queens – England – Biography – Juvenile
    literature
    3. Great Britain - History – Elizabeth, 1558-1603 –
    Juvenile literature
    I. Title
    942' .055'092

ISBN 07502 2290 5

Typeset in England by Joyce Chester
Printed and bound in Italy by
G. Canale & C.S.p.A Turin

Picture acknowledgements

The publishers gratefully acknowledge the following organizations for allowing their pictures to be reproduced in this book: Bridgeman Art Library/ Walker Art Gallery, (cover, main)/Christies Images 5/ Forbes Magazine Collection 9/ Houses of Parliament 11 (top)/ The Royal Cornwall Museum 17 (top)/ Berkeley Castle 18 (top)/ New York Public Library 20/ National Maritime Museum 21 (top)/ St Faith's Church 23/ Woburn Abbey 25 (title page), 27/ Burghley House Collection 26; Billie Love 8 (top); Hulton Getty 8 (bottom), 14 (bottom), 15, 17 (bottom), 19, 21, 29 (top); Mary Evans 11 (bottom), 13 (bottom), 28 (top); National Maritime Museum Picture Library (cover, background); Peter Newark 22 (top), 24 (top left); Robert Harding 4, 7 (bottom), 13 (top); Wayland/National Portrait Gallery 5 (top), 6, 7 (top), 14 (top), 10/ Niall McLeod 12/ 16, 18 (bottom), 24 (top right, bottom), 28 (bottom).

Find Wayland on the Internet at http://www.wayland.co.uk

All Wayland books encourage children to read and help them improve their literacy.

✓ The contents page, page numbers, headings and index help locate specific pieces of information.

✓ The glossary reinforces alphabetic knowledge and extends vocabulary.

✓ The further information section suggests other books dealing with the same subject.

✓ Find out more about how this book is specifically relevant to the National Literacy Strategy on page 31.

Contents

Life in Tudor England

After many years of wars and fighting, at last there was peace in England. Once again, English ships began to trade with other countries.

Tudor kings and queens ruled England four hundred years ago. King Henry VIII was a Tudor king.

A wealthy Tudor woman called Bess of Hardwick had this grand house built for her. ▼

Many people grew rich. They built large and beautiful houses. They wore fine clothes and ate huge meals. They sang, played music, and enjoyed life.

◀ King Henry VIII himself wrote and played music.

Tudor people loved music and dancing. ▼

Elizabeth is born

King Henry VIII wanted a son who would grow up to be the next king. He already had a daughter, Mary, with his first wife. But Henry was not satisfied. He divorced and married again. Henry was sure that his new wife, Anne Boleyn, would have a boy.

Mary was the daughter of King Henry and his first wife Catherine of Aragon. ▶

But Anne had a baby girl. They named her Elizabeth.

Three more years went by and Anne still did not have a baby boy. Henry grew tired of waiting.

The King's three children, Mary, Elizabeth and Edward, spent much of their childhood at Hatfield House, Hertfordshire. ▼

▲ Henry was charmed by Anne Boleyn's beauty.

The lonely princess

Henry had Anne arrested. She was taken to the Tower of London and executed. Princess Elizabeth was only 3 years old when she lost her mother.

◀ Princess Elizabeth aged 11. She must have been very uncomfortable in these clothes.

▲ Prisoners were taken by boat to Traitor's Gate and into the dreaded Tower of London.

▲ Henry enjoyed playing with his son in the royal nursery.

A few days later Henry married again. His new wife gave birth to a boy. They named him Edward.

Elizabeth had a lonely childhood. She spent most of her time apart from her father. She always looked forward to seeing her brother Edward though.

At that time, it was thought that girls were not able to learn. But Elizabeth was very clever. She loved to study. She learned Latin, Greek and other languages.

Time of change

When Henry died his son Edward became king. Sadly, Edward died when he was just 15 years old.

By now, Elizabeth was a young woman. With her long red hair and her lively ways people liked Elizabeth. But Mary, Elizabeth's older sister, became queen of England next.

◀ Edward VI was just 9 years old when he became king.

◀ Elizabeth was with Queen Mary as she was welcomed to the city of London as the new queen.

Mary had almost 300 Protestants put to death for their beliefs. ▼

Mary's religion was Catholic and she wanted everybody in England to be Catholic too. Most English people were Protestant and some were put to death. People became frightened of Mary.

Elizabeth is arrested

Elizabeth's religion was Protestant. Some people believed that if she were queen there would be peace. Mary worried that people wanted Elizabeth to be queen instead of her. So she had Elizabeth arrested and put in the Tower of London.

This painting shows soldiers arresting the young Princess Elizabeth. ▶

Elizabeth was frightened. Every day she thought about her own mother who had been executed in the Tower. She was afraid that she might be next.

The unhappy princess was shut away in the cold damp Tower. ▼

Elizabeth lived in fear of the axe. ▶

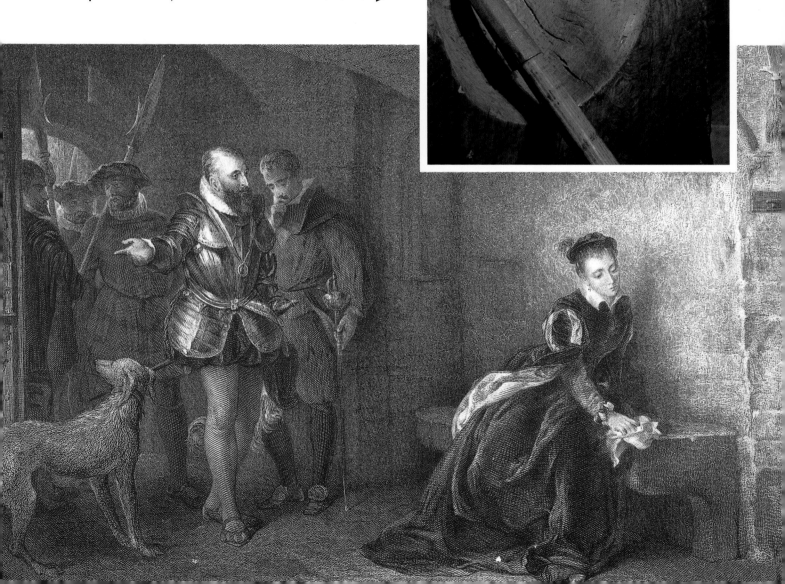

Elizabeth becomes queen

When Elizabeth was 25 years old Mary died. Elizabeth became Queen Elizabeth I. Her coronation was held in Westminster Abbey.

It was a happy day for England when Elizabeth was crowned Queen. ▶

Crowds filled the narrow streets of London as the Queen's coach went by. ▶

▲ Farm work was poorly paid. Many country people moved to the towns where they could earn more money.

Elizabeth wanted to make England a better place for everybody. This was not easy. Many people had moved to the towns to look for jobs. Towns had become crowded, dirty and unhealthy places in which to live.

The queen who never married

Elizabeth was young and pretty. She enjoyed jokes, and she had lots of friends. A few men became her special friends. Once or twice she even fell in love.

▲ Elizabeth loved to dance and party with her friends.

▲ The Queen and a friend play music at a picnic.

An ordinary woman would have married the man she loved. But Elizabeth was different. She knew that if she married her husband would want to share her power. She decided that she would never marry.

Queen Elizabeth and her Parliament. She enjoyed ruling over her people. ▶

Elizabeth's England

In spite of the crowds and the dirt, these were exciting times. Beautiful houses were built and unknown countries were explored. New music, poetry and plays were written.

Elizabeth playing the lute. Like her father King Henry VIII, she was a skilled musician. ▶

Another popular instrument, the harpsichord, had a keyboard like a piano. ▼

▲ A scene from Shakespeare's play *Twelfth Night*. It was performed at Elizabeth's court.

The playwright William Shakespeare became famous. People watched his plays at the new theatres which had been built in London. Elizabeth herself enjoyed his plays at court.

Exploring new lands

At that time, people did not know all the countries in the world. Explorers faced many dangers from storms, rocky coasts and unfriendly native people.

Sailors such as Francis Drake and Walter Raleigh were brave and explored new countries. They were looking for gold, precious stones and spices.

Elizabethan ships relied on wind for power so they were very slow. Drake's round-the-world voyage took nearly three years. ▼

Drake set out on a long voyage of discovery. He was the first English person to sail right around the world.

Francis Drake used this compass to help him find his way at sea.

They brought tobacco, coconuts and potatoes to Britain from America. English people had never smoked nor tasted these foods before.

Walter Raleigh landed in America and set up the Queen's flag. ▶

The Spanish Armada

Sometimes the English sea captains fought battles with Spanish ships. The King of Spain grew angry and started a war with England. He built a fleet of ships to carry his army across the sea. He called his ships the Armada.

The Spanish Armada sails to make war against England. ▶

▲ Before the battle started Elizabeth told the soldiers that she was ready to fight the Spanish and die along with her men.

The Spanish army hoped to take the English army by surprise but the people of England were ready to fight. Elizabeth was brave too. She visited her men before the battle began.

Victory

▲ Treasure from a sunken Spanish ship.

◀ Aboard the ship *Ark Royal*, English soldiers fight the Spanish.

These coins are part of the Armada treasure. ▼

The Spanish seamen had more ships than the English but the English ships were faster. The English also had bigger guns.

As soon as the Armada came into sight, the big English guns opened fire. Cannon balls crashed into the Spanish ships.

For a week the seamen fought furious battles. Spanish ships were damaged and sunk by the English. Many other Spanish ships were lost in terrible storms.

The rest of the Spanish ships returned to Spain. England had won the war and Elizabeth became even more popular.

▲ After England won the war, Elizabeth had this picture painted, with the ships of England and Spain in the background.

Lonely again

The years went by and Elizabeth grew older. One by one her good friends died. In front of other people she tried to be cheerful and strong. But secretly Elizabeth felt very lonely.

She still wore beautiful dresses and red wigs. But they could not hide her black teeth and her ageing skin.

▲ Elizabeth hated growing older.

Elizabeth grew fond of a young man called Robert who was the Earl of Essex. She believed that he cared for her too but he plotted against her. Elizabeth had him executed but this made her very sad.

Tall and handsome, Essex charmed the ageing queen. ▶

The death of Elizabeth

When the queen caught a cold nobody thought it was serious. But Elizabeth knew that she was dying. Before she died Elizabeth told her ministers that she wanted the King of Scotland, James VI, to be the next King of England.

◀ A messenger rode to Scotland to tell King James that he was to be the next king of England.

Queen Elizabeth's funeral. ▼

The Chariott drawne by foure Horses apon which Charret stood the Coffin conered wth purple Veluett and apon that the representation. The Canapy borne by six Knights.

In her last speech, Elizabeth told the people of England how much she loved them. People called this her Golden Speech, and her words were remembered long after her death.

The tomb of Queen Elizabeth I is in Westminster Abbey in London. ▶

Elizabeth was 70 years old when she died. She had been queen for forty-five years. In that time England had become a strong country and people remembered her as Good Queen Bess.

Timeline

1533   Elizabeth is born.
1558   Elizabeth becomes Queen of England.
1577–1580   Sir Francis Drake sails around the world.
1588   The Spanish Armada sails to make war with England.
1591   William Shakespeare begins to write plays and poetry.
1603   Elizabeth dies at the age of 70.

Glossary

Battles Fights between enemies.

Cannon balls Iron balls that were fired from large guns.

Catholic The Christian religion headed by the Pope in Rome.

Divorce To end a marriage.

Educated To know many things.

Executed To be put to death.

Greek The language spoken by the ancient Greeks.

Latin The language spoken by the ancient Romans.

Lute A musical instrument which looks similar to a small guitar.

Musical To play music well.

Parliament People who make decisions for the country.

Playwright Somebody who writes plays.

Protestant A branch of the Christian religion which broke away from the Catholics.

Theatre A place where actors perform plays.

Tower of London A building in London that was used as a prison. It is now a museum.

Victory To beat an enemy.

Voyage A long journey by sea.

Further information

Books to read

Famous People, Famous Lives: Elizabeth I by Harriet Castor (Franklin Watts, 1996)

Queen Elizabeth I by Dorothy Turner (Wayland, 1987, Reprinted 1994)

Tudors and Stuarts by Robert and Pat Unwin (Oxford University Press, 1994)

For advanced readers

Heritage: The Tudors by Robert Hull (Wayland, 1997)

Kings and Queens: Elizabeth I by Sheila Watson (Wayland, 1995)

Places to visit

Elizabeth's childhood home: Hatfield House, Hatfield, Hertfordshire.

Tower of London, Tower Hill, London.

Elizabeth's tomb: Westminster Abbey, London.

Use this book for teaching literacy

This book can help you in the literacy hour in the following ways:

☑ Children can re-tell the story of Queen Elizabeth I to give the main points in sequence and pick out significant incidents.

☑ Teaches children the stories behind part of our heritage, including the words we use.

☑ Children can use the story of Elizabeth and her times to write fictionalized accounts of, for example, the life of Elizabeth before she was queen.

Index

Numbers in **bold** refer to pictures and text.